Profiles in Greek and Roman Mythology

ACHILLES

Mitchell Lane
PUBLISHERS

P.O. Box 196
Hockessin, Delaware 19707
Visit us on the web: www.mitchelllane.com
Comments? email us: mitchelllane@mitchelllane.com

PROFILES IN GREEK AND ROMAN MYTHOLOGY

Titles in the Series

Profiles in Greek and Roman Mythology

ACHILLES

Tamra Orr

Mitchell Lane
PUBLISHERS

P.O. Box 196
Hockessin, Delaware 19707
Visit us on the web: www.mitchelllane.com
Comments? email us: mitchelllane@mitchelllane.com

Printing   1   2   3   4   5   6   7   8   9

Library of Congress Cataloging-in-Publication Data
Orr, Tamra.
  Achilles / by Tamra Orr.
      p. cm. — (Profiles in Greek and Roman mythology)
  Includes bibliographical references and index.
  ISBN 978-1-58415-706-9 (library bound)
  1. Achilles (Greek mythology)—Juvenile literature. 1. Title.
  BL820.A22O77 2009
  398.20938'01—dc22
                                                                                        2008020911

ABOUT THE AUTHOR: Tamra Orr is the author of more than 100 books for children of all ages. She lives in the Pacific Northwest with her four kids and husband. She has written more than a dozen books for Mitchell Lane Publishers, including *Jordin Sparks*, *Meet Our New Student From China*, *A Kid's Guide to Perennial Gardens*, *How to Convince Your Parents You Can Care for a Potbellied Pig*, and the five-volume Money Matters series.

PUBLISHER'S NOTE: This story is based on the author's extensive research, which she believes to be accurate. Documentation of such research is contained on page 45.

The internet sites referenced herein were active as of the publication date. Due to the fleeting nature of some web sites, we cannot guarantee they will all be active when you are reading this book.

To reflect current usage, we have chosen to use the secular era designations BCE ("before the common era") and CE ("of the common era") instead of the traditional designations BC ("before Christ") and AD (*anno Domini,* "in the year of the Lord").

TABLE OF CONTENTS

Profiles in Greek and Roman Mythology

Achilles' strength and confidence on the battlefield made him a hero to
admire—and to fear. His anger was his biggest enemy.

ACHILLES

CHAPTER 1

Ancient Heroes

Achilles (uh-KIH-leez) was furious. What were the gods doing? Until his argument with Greek commander Agamemnon, he had been unstoppable. He had won every battle he fought. His fleet-footed reputation was known far and wide. The Myrmidons (MEER-mih-dons), his soldiers who were fighting alongside the other Greek armies, looked up to him. He was the very definition of the word *hero* as he fought bravely in the Trojan War. Now the gods had heaped upon him a paralyzing grief. He had let his best friend, Patroclus—who had grown up with him in his father's house—take his place on the battlefield. It was just supposed to be a trick to rally the men. Instead it was the last thing Patroclus ever did, struck down in battle because the enemy believed he was actually Achilles—and because the god Apollo had allowed it.

The pain of Achilles' loss was unbearable, equaled only by the guilt. As his rage grew and shifted to a lust for revenge, he knew he must find Patroclus' killer and make him suffer. "Despite my anguish, I will beat it down," he says, "the fury mounting inside me, down by force. But now I'll go and meet that murderer head-on, that Hector who destroyed the dearest life I know."[1]

This was not the only time he renounced his anger. Achilles, one of the greatest heroes in Greek mythology, has been immortalized because of his rage. Homer's epic *The Iliad,* the poem of Ilium, or Troy, begins: "Rage—Goddess, sing the rage of Peleus' son Achilles."[2] This line refers to a quarrel between Achilles and his captain, Agamemnon, which so enrages the youth at the time that he refuses to fight. As the story progresses, spurred by gods and goddesses who have their own agendas, Achilles frequently squashes his anger in

order to get back to the battle. It is never easy for him though, and the consequences of his fury bring him more heartache and trouble than he could have imagined.

Explaining the World Around Them

To the ancient Greeks and Romans, the gods and heroes were very real. Although in modern times their stories might be compared to those of Spiderman, Batman, and Superman—swinging, jumping, and flying through the air to protect people in the name of justice—people in earlier cultures used myths not just for morality, but to explain their world.

The people of the past made up stories of powerful gods and goddesses who controlled many mysterious events. Storms, for example, were believed to be caused by an angry god looking for someone to punish. Each morning, the sun rose only because Helios, the god of light, drove the sun across the sky in a chariot. The gods and goddesses were exceptionally beautiful, powerful, and gifted. They brought riches and joy to the world—as well as pain and suffering. Besides everyday events, the stories about these otherworldly beings explained how the world was created, when and how people first appeared on the earth, how the world might end, and what happens after death. At all times, the gods and goddesses were in control, and for many people, that was a comforting thought.

The twelve main gods, called the Olympians, were believed to live on Mount Olympus, the highest mountain in Greece. They were Zeus (ZOOS), king of all the gods; Hera (HAYR-uh), his wife; Poseidon (poh-SY-dun), god of the sea; Hades (HAY-deez), god of the Underworld; Hestia (HES-tee-uh), goddess of the hearth, whose place on Olympus would be taken by Dionysus (dy-oh-NY-sus), god of wine and ecstasy; Ares (AIR-eez), god of war; Athena (uh-THEE-nuh), goddess of war and wisdom; Artemis (AR-tuh-mis), goddess of the hunt; her twin, Apollo, god of prophecy, music, and light; Aphrodite (aa-froh-DY-tee), goddess of love; Hermes (HUR-meez), messenger of the gods; and Hephaestus (heh-FES-tus), god of fire.

The gods and goddesses would often interact directly with mortals, and their unions would sometimes result in demigods (half-gods) and heroes. Achilles, for example, was the son of a sea nymph (or goddess) and a mortal. Hercules (HER-kyoo-leez) was another hero of divine parentage. Many of the heroes were known for honorable traits like courage, justice, love, honor, and faith. Their actions showed the importance of wisdom and honesty. The behavior of the gods and goddesses, on the other hand, was often dishonorable, featuring

High on Mount Olympus, a dozen mighty gods gathered to watch over—and often interfere with—the lives of the people below.

revenge and jealousy. Achilles showed a combination of negative and positive traits: anger, pride, and loyalty.

Typically, myths included the same elements over and over. Destiny and predictions were usually involved. Predictions were made by oracles—priests or priestesses who spoke on behalf of the gods.

These stories existed for countless years, passed along only through storytelling before they were written down. People of all ages would gather and listen to the tales of vengeful and compassionate gods, emotional and spiteful goddesses, and strong but brutal heroes. Sometimes the tales would be told by a professional storyteller. His voice would hold the audience closely, getting louder at the battles and softer at the deaths. These skillful speakers had to

have outstanding memories. Some stories took hours and hours to tell. With each telling, a detail here and there would change, and over time, the stories matured and expanded. They grew more intricate and, perhaps, more fantastic. In a day when there were no computers, televisions, telephones, or even books, listening to these tales was a favorite kind of entertainment.

Evidence of the power of myth in Greek and Roman societies has survived through the centuries. Myths were glorified in paintings, and captured on pottery and in sculptures. Magnificent temples and statues were built to honor different gods, goddesses, and heroes. People brought offerings of grain or animals to the temples, hoping that the gods would be grateful and, in return, treat them favorably. Festivals were held to honor the gods. Poets continued to recite their stories and legends to fascinated audiences. At home, the people offered prayers.

Homer

Eventually, people began writing down the stories. Around 800 BCE, Greek poet Homer wrote two epics, *The Iliad* and *The Odyssey*, that have survived to modern times. They center on the Trojan War and its aftermath—a short period of time in Greek and Roman history—and include the stories of the many heroes and deities that were a part of the battle. In the *Iliad,* the Greeks have been camped outside the walls of Troy for nine years. Beginning the action is the rage of Achilles.

Household Gods

Goddess Hestia

Gods and goddesses were a large part of Greek life, and they were honored in the household as well as in temples. For example, Hestia was the goddess of the hearth and protector of homes. She watched over the women as they baked the bread and prepared the family meals. Girls growing up in ancient Greece knew Hestia well, because much of their lives would revolve around the hearth and home. They spent their time taking care of the younger children and helping with chores.

The homes were small, usually with only two or three rooms and a courtyard in the middle. Larger homes sometimes offered a kitchen, bathing room, bedrooms, a room for the men, and a separate group of rooms for women known as the *gynaikonitis* (gye-nay-kuh-NYE-tiss). Girls in the country harvested foods such as olives and different fruits and vegetables. They made sure to stay out of the bright afternoon sun, though. Proper young ladies were not to be tan because that would indicate that they worked outdoors like slaves.

Mothers taught their daughters how to sew, spin, and weave to make clothing. In many homes, however, girls also had to help with chores. Greek families typically had female slaves to help them with cooking, cleaning, and carrying water. Male slaves sometimes acted as teachers to the youngest boys.

In the afternoon, women might go to visit another family nearby. They longed for the days when there would be a wedding or a funeral. Those were the only real times when the women were in charge. The festival of Dionysus was also a time for women to take a break from daily life.

Boys, on the other hand, spent a great deal of their waking hours working the land. Many families depended on their land to make the money they needed to survive. If they did not work their own land, they often worked for others richer and more powerful than they. The only free moments the boys had were when they were allowed to go on hunting trips or horseback rides with their fathers or older brothers.

In ancient Greece, Troy (in Phrygia) was known as Ilium. It was across the Aegean Sea from Helen's home in Sparta and Achilles' home in Phthia, an area of southern Thessaly (yellow). Peleus, the father of Achilles, was banished from Aegina (⬤), an island southwest of Athens. He moved to Phthia, and then to Iolcus (⬤).

ACHILLES

CHAPTER 2

Seeking Immortality

Like many heroes in the Greek and Roman myths, Achilles was the son of a deity and a mortal. Unlike other heroes, his father was a murderer.

Meet the Father

For many years, Achilles' father, Peleus (PEE-lee-us), led a life of great misfortune. At his mother's request, he and his brother Telamon (TEH-luh-mon) killed their half brother Phocus (FOH-kus). When their father, King Aeacus (EE-uh-kus), found out, he banished the two brothers from their island home of Aegina.

Telamon went to the island of Salamis and eventually became king there. Peleus went to Phthia, where he was welcomed by King Eurytion (yoo-RIH-shee-on). Not long after, he married the king's daughter, Antigone (an-TIH-guh-nee). They had a daughter named Polydora (pah-lee-DOOR-ah). All was well until Peleus was invited to go hunting for a wild boar with his father-in-law. The monstrous Calydonian boar was said to be from the Underworld and was sent to destroy as much of the land and its people as possible. Peleus spotted the boar and threw his spear. Instead of killing the monster, his spear killed the king. Once again, Peleus was exiled.

This time, Peleus traveled to Iolcus (eye-OL-kus), at the invitation of King Acastus (uh-KAS-tus). The king officially forgave Peleus for the murders. While things looked as if they would improve for Peleus at last, trouble was still ahead. The king's wife, Astydameia (ah-sty-duh-MAY-uh), fell in love with him. He was flattered—but not interested and said no thanks. This did not please the queen at all. Rejected and angry, she lashed out. First, she sent a message to

Antigone telling her that Peleus was going to marry King Acastus' daughter. The news so upset Antigone that she killed herself. Next, Astydameia accused Peleus of attacking her. King Acastus was furious. He had invited Peleus to his kingdom and forgiven him for his earlier crimes, and this was how he was repaid? He decided to kill Peleus for what he had done, but to avoid the wrath of the gods, he had to make it look like an accident.

First, he asked Peleus to go hunting with him in a forest filled with marauding centaurs. The men made a bet to see which one of them could kill the most animals. Peleus won, bringing back the tongue of each animal as proof. Later, when Peleus lay down to sleep, the king stole his sword and hid it. Then the king and his men left Peleus there while they returned to Iolcus. The king hoped that by leaving Peleus without any weapon, he would be attacked and killed by the centaurs or other wild animals that roamed the area.

Luckily for Peleus, when a centaur did find him, it was a wise and friendly one named Cheiron (KY-rohn). According to some stories, Cheiron was Peleus' grandfather. He helped Peleus find his sword and then took him to a place where he would be safe. The two became friends as Cheiron taught Peleus important skills and lessons.

Naturally, Peleus was outraged at how he had been tricked. He had done the honorable thing by refusing Astydameia, and still he was being punished. He wanted revenge—and he got it. Years later, he returned with an entire army and captured Iolcus, killing the queen and, in some tales, the king as well. He also acquired a new wife. The gods chose to award him by giving him the hand of Thetis (THEE-tiss)—a goddess who would prove to be far more challenging than anyone anticipated.

Meet the Mother

Thetis, a sea goddess, was the daughter of the old sea god Nereus (NEER-ee-oos) and the sea goddess Doris. In her younger days, Zeus

and Poseidon had both wanted to be with Thetis, but when an oracle predicted that her son would prove greater than his father, these gods lost interest. They decided that Thetis would be allowed to marry only a mortal instead of another god. They chose Peleus.

To win her, Peleus had to capture Thetis while she was sleeping in her cave. Once he had his arms around her, he had to hold on for dear life—for she had the ability to change shape. If he managed to get through all her transformations without letting go, she would be his.

First she turned into fire and then water and then wind. She became a lioness, a wolf, and a snake. Throughout it all, Peleus hung on. Finally Thetis agreed to marry him.

Time for a Wedding

Thetis and Peleus' wedding was a grand affair, with many gods and goddesses in attendance. Gifts were lavished on the couple: from Cheiron, a stout spear polished by Athena and tipped with a blade

The Wedding of Peleus and Thetis, painted by Cornelis van Haarlem in 1593. Peleus and Thetis were married on Mount Pelion, which was home to the centaurs.

forged by Hephaestus; from Poseidon, two immortal horses, Xanthus (ZAN-thus) and Bailus; and from Hephaestus, a magnificent suit of armor. However, one deity was not invited: Eris (AYR-iss), the goddess of discord. That mistake would have disastrous effects for years. Angry, Eris crashed the wedding. She threw a golden apple onto the ground, inscribed "to the fairest." Three goddesses began fighting over the apple: Hera, Athena, and Aphrodite. To determine who was "the fairest," Paris, the prince of Troy, was named judge of the contest. Each goddess tried to win his vote. Hera tempted him with unlimited power. Athena offered him victory in battle. It was Aphrodite, however, who won. She offered him the love of the most beautiful woman in the world, Helen. She did not mention that Helen was already married to King Menelaus (meh-nuh-LAY-us)

The Judgment of Paris, painted by Peter Paul Rubens in 1636. Paris' difficult decision had repercussions throughout the Greek world.

of Sparta. Paris traveled to Sparta soon after to collect Helen. He stole her from her castle and left for Troy. The insult to Menelaus sparked the Trojan War.

Becoming a Family

Thetis and Peleus had seven sons. The last one was Achilles. Thetis, frustrated because she couldn't marry a god, wanted to make her children immortal. She covered each baby in special oil known as ambrosia, and then set the child in the fire. The ceremony would burn off the mortal parts and leave the immortal side. What happened to the first six children is not really known. Some stories say they did not survive the immortality process. Others say Thetis killed them because she was so unhappy about being married to a mere mortal. In the end, the only child left was Achilles.

Thetis was determined to make the immortality process work on Achilles. "Unequal is thy birth, my son, and only on your mother's side is the way of death barred for thee," she said to him.[1] At last, with Achilles, Thetis succeeded. Some myths say that the fire trick worked. The Roman version says that she dipped him in the river Styx, which divided the living and the dead. Either way, Achilles was now immortal—except for one spot on the back of his heel. This is either where Peleus pulled Achilles out of the fire or

Thetis Dipping Achilles into the Styx (detail), painted by Peter Paul Rubens in 1625. As Thetis dips her son into the river, she holds him by the heel.

The Education of Achilles by James Barry. Achilles learned many skills from Cheiron, including how to play the lyre.

where Thetis held the boy as she lowered him into the water. It was the only spot on Achilles' body that could be injured—and lead to his death.

Even though Thetis had gotten what she wanted—an immortal son—she was still angry with Peleus and hated her life with him. At last, she simply walked away from her family and went back to live in the sea. Peleus did not know how he was going to raise his young son all by himself. Then he remembered who had helped to teach him in the past—Cheiron. With relief, Peleus turned Achilles over to the centaur. Now he knew his son was in trusted hands.

Cheiron

When Peleus was saved by Cheiron, most centaurs were not known for their kindness toward humans. Part human and part horse, these creatures tended to be violent and avoided gods and heroes as much as possible. Many myths show centaurs as rough, loud, angry, and often murderous. Cheiron, however, was the oldest and wisest of them all. Along with being a centaur, he was also immortal, a half brother to Zeus. He had been fathered by Cronus, who had taken the shape of a horse when his wife came looking for him as he slept with Cheiron's mother, Philyra.

Cheiron was not only a great teacher, but a father as well. He had a daughter named Endeis. When she grew to be a woman, she married Aeacus and, in turn, became mother to Peleus and Telamon. When Cheiron saved Peleus from almost certain death and helped him get his sword back, he was helping his own grandson. Cheiron also helped raise Achilles and other heroes, including Jason and Hercules. He taught them many different skills, from survival to courage. Classics scholar A.R. Hope Moncrieff wrote that Cheiron was "master of the healing art, and this they learned. . . . He taught them to sing, to make music, to bear themselves gracefully in the dance, but also to run, box, wrestle, to climb the dizzy rocks, and to hunt wild beasts in the mountain forests, laughing at all dangers. . . . They grew up under the care of Cheiron to be both skilful and strong, modest as well as brave, and fitted to rule by having rightly known to obey."[2]

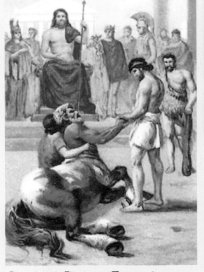

Cheiron was known as a great healer, but he was accidentally hit by Hercules with an arrow dipped in the Hydra's deadly blood. As an immortal, he did not die from the wound but lived in terrible pain. Finally, a Titan named Prometheus offered to take the place of Cheiron, allowing him to die. To honor the centaur, Zeus placed his spirit in the sky as the constellation Centaurus.

Death of Cheiron. Even when faced with a lifetime of torture, Cheiron was generous and kind.

Thetis Takes Achilles from the Centaur Cheiron, painted by Pompeo Batoni in 1770.
When Thetis hears Achilles may be called to go to Troy, she decides to hide him from
his fellow Greeks, who need him to win the Trojan War.

ACHILLES

Even though Thetis had walked away from her family life, she never stopped thinking and worrying about her son. Along with being a sea nymph and a shape shifter, she was also a prophet. A vision told her that Achilles had two possible futures: He would either join in the battle during the Trojan War and become a huge hero—but die at a young age—or he would live a long and healthy life if he just stayed away from the war and fame. As a mother, the choice was easy. She was going to do everything possible to keep her son out of the war.

Unfortunately, Thetis was not the only one who knew this information. When the Trojan War began over the kidnapping of Helen, the best warriors were called upon to support the Greek side. The seer Calchas (KAL-kus) had told many people that the Greeks would never be able to take Troy if they did not have Achilles by their side. Word got out that he was essential to the war effort—but where was he?

Undercover!

Clever Thetis had come up with a daring idea to keep him from serving in the war. She and Peleus sent him to live in the court of King Lycomedes (ly-KOH-mee-deez) on the island of Scyros. They dressed him in skirts and scarves so that he would look like a girl, and gave him the name Pyrrha (PEER-uh). They hid him inside the same building as all the king's daughters. No one would think to look for him there, they thought.

In some ways, they were right. He was hidden there for a long time, fathering at least one child, Neoptolemus (nee-up-TAH-luh-mus),

with a daughter of the king. Finally Odysseus (oh-DIH-see-us), a Greek leader who was known for being clever, thought of a way to find Achilles. He tracked the boy to Scyros but could not find where he was hiding. Finally, he figured out that only one place had not been searched: the room where the royal daughters were kept.

This time Odysseus put on a disguise. He knew that Achilles would never show himself if he recognized who he was. Dressed as a peddler, Odysseus entered the king's courtyard with trinkets to sell. He put out pieces of jewelry and bright, shiny cloth. The girls swarmed all over it. Over to the side, he added some weapons, including a sword. At his signal, one of his men blew a war horn, indicating that the kingdom was under attack. While the girls scattered in fright, one among them ripped off his scarves, grabbed the

The Discovery of Achilles among the Daughters of Lycomedes, painted by Jan de Bray in 1664. Achilles reveals himself by grabbing a sword planted by the clever Odysseus.

sword, and turned to fight. Of course, that was Achilles. Odysseus smiled. His trick had worked perfectly.

After a long talk, Odysseus finally convinced Achilles to sail to Troy with him. Achilles knew that agreeing would bring about his death. He told Odysseus:

> "Mother tells me,
> the immortal goddess Thetis with her glistening feet,
> that two fates bear me on the day of death.
> If I hold out here and I lay siege to Troy,
> my journey home is gone, but my glory never dies.
> If I voyage back to the fatherland I love,
> my pride, my glory dies . . .
> true, but the life that's left me will be long,
> the stroke of death will not come on me quickly."[1]

Choosing between glory and a long life was not an easy decision to make.

Divine Intervention?

Preparing for war, Achilles inherited his parents' wedding presents —the magnificent armor forged by Hephaestus, Cheiron's sturdy staff, and the two immortal horses. These horses, Xanthus and Bailus, could see what was to come and could speak to their owners. Achilles had known that one day these horses would be his, because Cheiron had told him long before: "For although you have been taught by me . . . the art of horsemanship and are suited to such a horse as I, some day you shall ride on Xanthus and Bailus; and you shall take many cities and slay many men."[2]

Achilles remembered this prediction as he headed for war. As soon as he reached a ship to take him to Troy, he was made an admiral. This gave him power over the men—but did nothing for his ability to navigate. The fleet headed across the Aegean Sea, only to

Automedon, the charioteer for Achilles, holds Achilles' powerful horses Xanthus and Bailus.

lose its way and accidentally land in Mysia. The Greeks tried to pillage a city, but they were attacked by Telephus (TEH-luh-fus), the husband of one of Paris' sisters. Achilles wounded Telephus and then returned to the sea. Telephus had a problem, however. He had been told by an oracle that if he was ever wounded in battle, he could be healed only by the one who had injured him. That was Achilles! Telephus sailed across the sea in pursuit of the hero.

He finally caught up with Achilles, but Achilles claimed he knew nothing about healing. Finally, with the help of Odysseus, they figured out that it was not actually Achilles that had done the wounding, but his spear. They rubbed the spearhead into the wound and it worked! Telephus was fine. He had to pay a price, however. In return for being healed, he had to promise Achilles to guide them to Troy. Achilles did not want the fleet to get lost again!

The Journey Begins

On the way to Troy, the fleet had to stop twice. The first time was on Aulis, where the ship's sails could not catch a favorable wind. Calchas told the men that Artemis was angry with Agamemnon and would only allow the winds to blow if they sacrificed his daughter, Iphigenia (ih-fih-jih-NY-uh). Torn between failing to get his troops to Troy in time and losing his daughter, Agamemnon chose the latter. He sent a letter to Iphigenia stating that he wanted her to come to him in Aulis because he had promised her hand in marriage to the warrior Achilles. He kept this lie to himself, not even letting Achilles know of his deception.

Once Iphigenia arrived with her mother, Clytemnestra (kly-tem-NES-truh), the plan became clear. First Clytemnestra begged her husband to spare their daughter's life, and then Iphigenia begged as well. Calchas stated that if Iphigenia did not agree to being killed, her whole family would be stoned to death by the angry army. Agamemnon turned his head from the women and agreed to the sacrifice.

Achilles was understandably upset when he discovered that his name had been used against this young woman. He offered to marry her to help her escape. Filled with a sense of nobility and a dedication to the greater cause, however, Iphigenia agreed to be sacrificed. Just as Calchas was beginning to slash the young girl's neck, she vanished. In her place was a deer or young bull. The men

The Sacrifice of Iphigenia, painted by Jan Steen in 1671. As Agamemnon looks on in despair and a young boy turns away in tears, the end of Iphigenia seems inevitable.

suspected it was Artemis who had stepped in at the last moment to save the girl's life. Soon after, the winds began to blow, and the fleet was able to move on.

The second stop was at the island of Tenedos (TEH-neh-dos), near Troy. Determined to kill as many Trojan leaders as he could, Achilles killed the king, Tenes. His mother had warned him not to do so—she told him that Tenes' father, Apollo, would avenge his son's death someday, but Achilles ignored this warning.

Achilles, who was hailed a hero, was quite brutal in war. Before arriving in Troy, he led his forces to conquer a dozen Phrygian cities by sea and another dozen by land. He drove the Trojan leader Aeneas from the battle and then tormented and terrorized more than fifty people in the family of Trojan King Priam (PRY-um). Some were captured and ransomed. Others were sold as slaves. Women were kidnapped and forced to travel with the Greek army.

When Agamemnon took as his prize a Trojan girl named Chryseis (krih-SAY-is), her father Chryses (KRY-sees) came to the leader and asked to buy her back. Agamemnon refused and told him to leave, then threatened to hurt him if he returned. As a priest of Apollo, Chryses prayed to the god to send a plague to the Greek men. Soon, soldiers and horses began dying. To ease the suffering of his troops, Agamemnon was forced to return Chryseis to her father. "I am willing to give her back," he admitted, "even so, if that is best for all. What I really want is to keep my people safe, not see them dying."[3]

Although he agreed to return the girl, he felt as commander he shouldn't be deprived of his war prize. He demanded to have Achilles' girl, Briseis (brih-SAY-iss), instead. Agamemnon may have appeased the "god of the plague"[4]—but he was about to have a feud with Achilles that would greatly impede the war effort.

The God of Fire

Hephaestus was the Greek god of fire. In Roman myth, he was known as Vulcan. He controlled the blacksmith's fire as well as the volcano's fire, which he used for a furnace. Although he was the son of Zeus and Hera, he was born weak and lame.

As a child, he was thrown off Mount Olympus. According to one version of the myth, his mother thought he was ugly, so she tossed him off. He was rescued by the nymphs Thetis and Eurynome and taken to a cave, where he was raised with care. Later, after he'd gone back to Olympus, Zeus threw him over because he sided with his mother during a husband-and-wife quarrel. Hephaestus fell for days before he landed in the sea. He then lived on Lemnos until he recovered.

Hephaestus

Some myths say that this god wanted to marry the goddess Athena, but she refused because of how he looked. Some say he married the goddess of love, Aphrodite, but caught her cheating on him with Ares, the god of war. He trapped them in a magic chain-link net he had created, and called all the gods to come witness their deceit. Instead of punishing them, however, the gods just laughed at the couple and let them go.

Hephaestus' greatest skill was fashioning things out of various materials. Metal was his favorite. He made Zeus' thunderbolts and a shield for Athena. He made Eros' arrows and the chariot that the sun god Helios (or Apollo) rode across the sky. He made Achilles' invincible armor. In the *Iliad,* Homer describes this fire god dramatically:

"[He] heaved up from his anvil block—his immense hulk
hobbling along but his shrunken legs moved nimbly.
He swung the bellows aside and off the fires,
gathered the tools he'd use to weld the cauldrons . . .
Then he sponged off his brow and both burly arms,
his massive neck and shaggy chest, pulled on a shirt
and grasping a heavy staff, Hephaestus left his forge
and hobbled on."[5]

Achilles by Johann Heinrich Wilhelm Tischbein. Although Achilles won Briseis as a war-prize, the two fell in love and lived as husband and wife. When Agamemnon demanded that Achilles turn her over to him, Achilles and Briseis pined for each other.

ACHILLES

CHAPTER 4

The Raging Battle

Although he argued with his commander, Achilles could not keep Agamemnon from taking Briseis. He complained to Agamemnon:

> "My honors never equal yours
> Whenever we sack some wealthy Trojan stronghold—
> my arms bear the brunt of the raw, savage fighting,
> true, but when it comes to dividing up the plunder,
> the lion's share is yours and back I go to my ships,
> clutching some scrap, some pittance that I love,
> when I have fought to exhaustion."[1]

He was so angry about the insult, he threatened to leave altogether and go home to Phthia. As his anger mounted, he was tempted to run the commander through with his sword, but was stopped just in time by Athena, who yanked his hair from behind and said, "Down from the skies I come to check your rage if only you will yield." He complied, "though his heart [broke] with fury."[2]

Achilles sheathed his sword, but instead of checking his rage, Homer says, he "rounded on Agamemnon once again, lashing out at him, not relaxing his anger for a moment."[3] After a venomous argument, Achilles refused to fight for the Greeks, or even to come out of his tent. He encouraged his men not to fight either. Without his power, the Greek army could not win against Troy.

Pride Before a Fall

Odysseus and others tried to convince Achilles to rejoin them on the battlefield, but his stubborn pride would not allow it. He was offered

women, riches, and other treasures. Agamemnon even offered to give Briseis back. He claimed he had not touched her in any way. Every offer was refused. Achilles could be terribly stubborn if he wanted to be. He took the time to pray to his mother over this matter as well. He asked Thetis to persuade Zeus to let the Trojans keep winning for a while. He hoped this would embarrass Agamemnon and make himself more sorely missed. She agreed, and for a while, the Trojans were definitely on the winning side of the war.

The Greeks began to lose faith in their battle. Without Achilles to encourage them and lead them confidently into each fight, they grew worried. Finally, Achilles' lifetime friend and close companion Patroclus had an idea. After berating his friend for having such a vile

Minerva Preventing Achilles from Killing Agamemnon, from "The Iliad" by Homer, painted in 1757 by Giovanni Battista Tiepolo. Achilles is so angry at Agamemnon for taking Briseis, he wants to kill him. Athena (known to the Romans as Minerva) stops him just in time by grabbing his hair from behind.

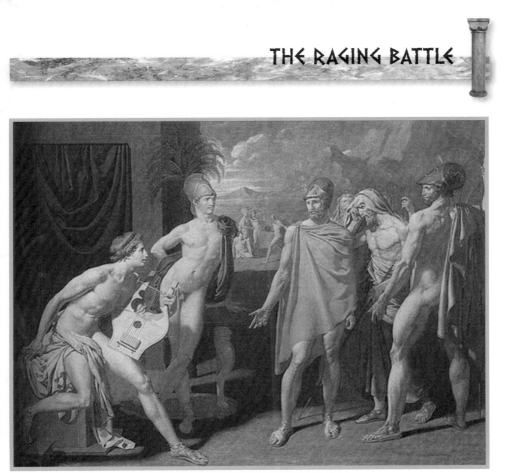

The Ambassadors of Agamemnon in the Tent of Achilles, painted in 1801 by Jean August Dominique Ingres. In Book 9 of *The Iliad,* Achilles (left) is still angry with Agamemnon for stealing Briseis. Instead of fighting, he lounges in his tent, playing the lyre for Patroclus (who is wearing Achilles' helmet). Odysseus (center), Phoenix, and Ajax must convince Achilles to return to battle.

temper, he persuaded Achilles to let him borrow his armor and go out on the field. He hoped that this would fool the men into thinking he was Achilles and cheer them up, perhaps inspiring them to return to battle with confidence. He also hoped the Trojans would believe that Achilles was back and rapidly retreat. In Book 16 of the *Iliad,* Patroclus says to his friend,

> "Pray god such anger never seizes *me,* such rage you nurse.
> Cursed in your own courage! . . .
> your temper's so relentless.

But still, if deep down some prophecy makes you balk,
some doom your noble mother revealed to you from Zeus,
well and good; at least send *me* into battle, quickly.
Let the whole Myrmidon army follow my command—
I might bring some light of victory to our Argives!
And give me your own fine armor to buckle on my back,
so the Trojans might take *me* for you, Achilles . . ."[4]

Achilles agreed to let him go, but unfortunately, Patroclus got caught up in the role he was playing and began killing as many Trojans as he could reach. His frenzy would prove to be fatal.

As Patroclus was fighting, Apollo struck him on the back and knocked off his helmet. The god then stripped the rest of the armor off him, and in seconds the soldier was wounded. Hector, son of King Priam, brother to Paris, and commander of the Trojan forces, saw the unguarded soldier. Without hesitation, he dealt the final blow. As Patroclus died, Apollo smiled; he had just taken his first step in avenging the death of his son Tenes at Achilles' hands. His next step would have to wait a little longer.

Girding for Battle

Achilles was overwhelmed with grief and almost lost his mind over his dear friend's death. He had known Patroclus since they were boys, and they had been very close. He laments to Thetis:

"O dear mother, true! All those burning desires
Olympian Zeus has brought to pass for me—
but what joy to me now? My dear comrade's dead—
Patroclus—the man I loved beyond all other comrades,
loved as my own life—I've lost him—Hector's killed him . . .
My spirit rebels—I've lost the will to live,
to take my stand in the world of men—unless,
before all else, Hector's battered down by my spear
and gasps away his life, the blood-price for Patroclus."[5]

32

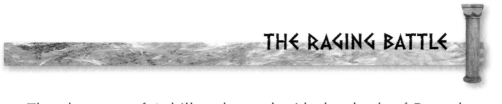
The character of Achilles changed with the death of Patroclus. While earlier he had been both a strong soldier and a decent person, his vengeance began to consume him. He said to his mother, who was still doing everything she could to keep her son out of the war,

Thetis Bringing the Armor to Achilles by Benjamin West, 1804. Achilles, mourning the death of Patroclus, turns to Thetis as she hands him the magnificent armor that was forged by Hephaestus.

"Don't try to hold me back from the fighting, Mother, love me as you do, you can't persuade me now."[6]

When Thetis realized that her son would fight in the war after all, she asked Hephaestus, the god of fire, to make Achilles another suit of armor that would protect him from any kind of weapon. Because she had helped raise Hephaestus after he was cast from Mount Olympus as a baby, he was happy to help her.

Hephaestus fashioned for him a shield of metal five layers thick, featuring earth and sea and sky, with lively scenes of cities and feasting and warring and farming—far more populous than could possibly fit on a battle shield, unless it were forged by the god of fire. After the "indestructible shield," he "made Achilles a breastplate brighter than gleaming fire," a helmet, and greaves to protect his shins.[7]

As Achilles' anger flared once more, he stared at the glorious armor. According to Homer: "the more he gazed, the deeper his anger went, his eyes flashing under his eyelids, fierce as fire."[8] Finally, Achilles was ready to fight.

Back Under Control

Renouncing his rage once more, Achilles told Agamemnon:

> "Enough! . . .
> Despite my anguish I will beat it down,
> the fury mounting inside me, down by force.
> Now, by god, I call a halt to all my anger—
> it's wrong to keep on raging, heart inflamed forever."[9]

Despite his declaration—which he makes several times throughout the *Iliad*—he was out for revenge and unstoppable. He declared, "I have no taste for food—what I really crave is slaughter and blood and the choking groans of men."[10] Fortified by nectar and ambrosia, he killed as many Trojans as he could, tossing them in the river Scamander as he went. This made the river god angry. He did not want his waters filled with corpses, so he flooded the battlefield. Achilles was almost drowned, but Hephaestus saw what was happening and dried up the water with one of his flames.

Achilles was so determined to get revenge that he almost singlehandedly wiped out the Trojan troops. Finally he came face to face with Hector. When Hector saw him, he turned and ran. He knew Achilles' reputation. Achilles chased him around the entire city, three times—until Zeus with his scales weighed the fate of these heroes, and Hector's heavy measure foretold his death. Apollo, who had been helping Hector flee, left his side. Hector, in the armor he had stripped from Patroclus, stopped to face his pursuer.

Both men hurled their spears. Achilles missed, but Athena brought his spear back to him. Hector hit his adversary's shining shield, lost his spear, and was left with just a sword. As he rushed the mighty Achilles, his neck was sliced by his opponent's spear, gift of Cheiron to Peleus and then to Peleus' son. With his dying breath, Hector begged Achilles to accept a ransom from his family for his body so that he could be properly buried.

Achilles stared at Hector and said in a rage,

"Beg no more, you fawning dog—begging me by my parents!
Would to god my rage, my fury would drive me now
to hack your flesh away and eat you raw—
such agonies you have caused me! Ransom?
No man alive could keep the dog-packs off you,
not if they haul in ten, twenty times that ransom
and pile it here before me and promise fortunes more. . . .
The dogs and birds will rend you—blood and bone!"[11]

Hector died, and Achilles tied his corpse behind his chariot and dragged his body around the walls of Troy every day for twelve days. This was the ultimate humiliation for a leader as brave and well-known as Hector. Meanwhile, Achilles honored Patroclus' death by holding athletic competitions and handing out prizes to all of his men.

This act of disrespect toward Hector truly angered the gods. They forced Achilles to turn Hector's body over to King Priam and the rest

Triumph of Achilles, painted in 1892 by Franz Matsch, shows Achilles dragging Hector's body behind his chariot. Dishonoring the great warrior offended even the gods. They made sure that Hector's corpse was not damaged during the twelve days of Achilles' madness.

Hector's corpse is brought back to Troy for burial, as shown on a Roman sarcophagus (about 200 CE).

of his family for a proper burial. Achilles agreed to do it. When Priam arrived, the two embraced for a moment, and Priam said, "I have endured what no one on earth has ever done before—I put to my lips the hands of the man who killed my son."[12] Together, Achilles and Priam wept over the tragic sacrifices of war. Showing a return to good manners, Achilles graciously allowed Priam to give Hector the burial he deserved.

Achilles achieved many things during the Trojan War, including learning how to rein in his hostility and set his anger aside to do whatever needed to be done at the moment. He honored and avenged his friend Patroclus and proved himself a powerful soldier and leader. He also revealed a capacity for great compassion when he returned Hector's body. Now, just as his destiny had predicted, the time he had left was short.

"The Face That Launched a Thousand Ships"

Helen of Troy, who was so beautiful that she created a decade-long war, was one of the daughters of Zeus. Her mother was Leda, and legend states that she was born from an egg, along with twin brothers Castor and Polydeuces, and sister Clytemnestra, who would marry Agamemnon.

From an early age, Helen was incredibly beautiful. Before she was even ten years old, she was carried off by Theseus. Her brothers rescued her. Men from age 29 to 99 courted her, and her mortal father, Tyndareus, did not know what to do about it. He was afraid that if he picked out a husband for her, it would anger all the other men. Finally, clever Odysseus suggested that all the men should not only agree to accept whoever Helen chose, but to come to this man's aid if he ever needed it. Helen chose Menelaus, a man of wealth and power.

Helen of Troy

Later, when Aphrodite promised Paris the love of the most beautiful woman in the world, there was no doubt she meant Helen. When Paris kidnapped her, Menelaus called in the oath her former suitors had made, and they set off for Troy to bring her back. Helen's actions during the war made it clear that she was happy being with Paris—although she refused his advances in the *Iliad,* Aphrodite made her fall in love with him. Helen often helped him win battles against the same men who were fighting to rescue her.

Once the war was over, Menelaus forgave his wife and took her back to Sparta, a trip that took eight years. She appears later in Homer's *Odyssey* as the queen of Sparta. There are two stories about how she eventually died. Some say she hanged herself out of guilt. Others state that Thetis killed her for indirectly causing her son's death.

Centuries after Homer, Christopher Marlowe wrote of Helen in *Doctor Faustus:* "Was this the face that launch'd a thousand ships,/ and burnt the topless towers of Ilium—/ Sweet Helen, make me immortal with a kiss."[13]

Achilles and Penthesileia, carved on a third-century sarcophagus in Rome.
Achilles holds the dying queen after he has delivered the fatal blow.

ACHILLES

CHAPTER 5

The End of Achilles

Much of what we know of the life of Achilles comes from Homer's *Iliad,* which ends with Hector's funeral and with Achilles still alive. From other sources, we find out that after the death of Hector, battle resumed in the Trojan War. Amazon and Assyrian reinforcements arrived to help the Trojans.

Amazon warrior

The Amazons, a nation of women, were led to Troy by Queen Penthesileia (pen-theh-sih-LEE-uh), daughter of the war god Ares. These women were tough—they were warlike and always carried weapons. Penthesileia succeeded in killing many Greeks with her lethal spear. Eventually, Achilles heard about this strong and fearsome woman. He began looking for her. When he spotted her, he did not hesitate to kill her. She was an amazing fighter, but no match for the mighty Achilles. As she was dying, he took off her armor and saw that this Amazon queen was young and extremely beautiful. The two looked into each other's eyes and immediately fell in love. He regretted what he had done, but it was too late.

The Assyrians Arrive

The Trojans were also helped by the Assyrians, a group of people from what is now Iraq, Iran, and Turkey. They were led by a prince named Memnon (MEM-non). When he and his men surrounded

Nestor, a Greek leader, Nestor's son Antilochus (an-TIL-uh-kus) stepped in to save him. The boy was killed. In his grief, Nestor asked his friend Achilles to avenge his son's death.

It was a hard decision for the warrior to make. He knew from his mother's visions that he was supposed to die soon after Memnon. If he killed the leader, he would be hastening his own death. Despite this, he wanted to honor Antilochus' death, so he agreed. After a vicious duel, he killed Memnon, and the Trojans retreated. Without their leader, they no longer felt they could continue to fight.

Achilles chased the soldiers into Troy, where an arrow pierced his ankle, and he died.

Apollo shows Paris where to aim his arrow in *The Death of Achilles* by Peter Paul Rubens, created around 1632.

A Time of Death

The death of Achilles was a simple one compared to the wild life the warrior had led. Apollo, in his obsession to avenge his son's death, told Paris the one place where Achilles could be injured— the back of his heel. Paris picked up his bow and arrow and shot Achilles in the heel, precisely where Apollo had instructed.

When Achilles died, the Trojans and Greeks fought fiercely over his body. The great soldier Ajax was finally able to carry his corpse back to camp while Odysseus kept the Trojans at bay. The body of Achilles was put on a funeral pyre and burned. Thetis and her forty-nine sea sisters, the Nereids (NEER-ee-idz), rose out of the water and took his ashes. They put them in a golden urn, mixing in ashes from

Patroclus, and either took them back down into the sea or buried them alongside the remains of Antilochus.

According to some myths, after death, Achilles went to the White Isle and lived there in complete happiness. However, in Homer's *Odyssey*, a story that takes place after the *Iliad*, Achilles was not happy in the afterlife. When he meets Odysseus there, he tells his friend:

> "Let me hear no smooth talk
> of death from you, Odysseus, light of councils.
> Better, I say, to break sod as a farm hand
> for some poor country man, on iron rations,
> than lord it over all the exhausted dead."[1]

Awarding Achilles' Armor

Now that Achilles was gone, what was to happen to his invincible armor? It was decreed that it should go to the best Greek warrior. Odysseus and Ajax both felt they deserved it. Some stories say they fought for it, while others suggest they played checkers for it. Another version says they ran in athletic games, with Trojans acting as judges! In the end, Odysseus won. Ajax was angry. He planned to wait for Odysseus to fall asleep and then kill him and steal the armor back. However, the goddess Athena was watching over Odysseus, and when she saw Ajax approaching, she put him under a spell. Instead of killing people, the warrior began killing the sheep and cows that were to feed

A replica of Achilles' shield

the army. When the spell ended and he realized what he had done, Ajax was so upset that he used Hector's sword to kill himself.

What actually happened to the armor is unsure. One myth states that it was buried with Ajax. Another states that Odysseus gave it to Achilles' son, Neoptolemus.

Fate and Necessity

Achilles was certainly considered to be a great warrior. He showed no fear on the battlefield, and when someone he cared about was wronged, he did not hesitate to avenge that wrong, even when it meant hastening his own death. Although he was sometimes brutal in war, that was exactly what was called for in a Greek hero. He did what was necessary to win, even if it was violent and cruel.

Achilles is remembered by his most vulnerable spot. The term *Achilles' heel* is used for the tendon that runs along the back of the ankle. It links the muscles of the calf to the heel bone. That tendon is not necessarily weak, but it can be injured easily. The term is also used to indicate a person's overall weakness. Both terms are based on the mythical warrior of long ago who was nearly immortal— but for that one small spot.

Back view of statue, detail

Dying Achilles
at Achilleion
in Corfu, Greece

Beyond the *Iliad*

After the *Iliad,* Homer wrote the *Odyssey.* This epic tale starts ten years after the Trojan War has ended, and yet Odysseus has still not returned to his kingdom in Ithaca. His family is eager for him to come home. Many believe he is dead, including the hundreds of suitors who want to marry his wife, Penelope. As the suitors wait for Penelope's answer, they are eating Odysseus out of house and home.

On his journey, Odysseus stopped at several places and recounted the incredible adventures he had had since Hector's death at Troy. He told of the ingenious idea he and Athena had crafted to create a magnificent wooden horse large enough for soldiers to hide inside. Thinking it was a gift from the losing Greeks, the Trojans pulled it into the center of their city to remind them of their victory. Once the Trojans were asleep, the Greeks piled out of the horse and slaughtered their enemies.

Odysseus also told the story of when he was imprisoned on a sea nymph's island, and Zeus arranged his rescue. Once freed, he grabbed a ship and headed home, only to be stopped by a storm sent by Poseidon. Athena stepped in to help, and Odysseus ended up on Scheria, home of the Phaeacians (fee-AY-shuns). Their princess, Nausicaa (NAW-sih-kuh), guaranteed that she would help him get home if only he would stay long enough to tell them of his adventures. The stories were very exciting as he described his trip to the Land of the Lotus Eaters, his battle with a Cyclops, and his temptation by the singing Sirens, women of the sea who lured men to watery deaths.

True to their word, the Phaeacians delivered Odysseus safely to Ithaca. Once there, he disguised himself as a beggar and mingled with the suitors in his house. A contest was called to see who should win Penelope's hand. The man had to string Odysseus' bow and shoot straight through the holes in a line of ax heads. Odysseus won the contest easily and killed the suitors. The word *odyssey* has come to mean "a great journey."

Odysseus
presenting
wine to the
Cyclops

Chapter 1. Ancient Heroes

1. Homer, *The Iliad,* translated by Robert Fagles (New York: Penguin Books: 1990), Book 18, lines 132–136, p. 471.

2. Ibid., Book 1, line 1, p. 77.

Chapter 2. Seeking Immortality

1. Statius, *Achilleid*, translated by J. H. Mozley, Loeb Classical Library (Cambridge, Massachusetts: Harvard University Press; London: William Heinemann Ltd., 1928), Book 1, line 256; online at http://www.theoi.com/Text/StatiusAchilleid1A.html

2. Moncreiff, A.R. Hope, *Classic Myth and Legend* (London, England: Gresham Publishing Company, undated), accessed at http://www.merrynjose.com/artman/publish/article_127.shtml

Chapter 3. From Disguise to War

1. Homer, *The Iliad,* translated by Robert Fagles (New York: Penguin Books: 1990), Book 9, lines 497–505, p. 265.

2. *Elder Philostratus, Younger Philostratus, Callistratus,* translated by Arthur Fairbanks, Loeb Classical Library, Volume 256 (London, England: William Heinneman, 1931), Book 19, line 408.

3. Homer, Book 1, lines 136–138, p. 81.

4. Ibid., Book 1, line 45.

5. Ibid., Book 18, lines 479–488, p. 481.

Chapter 4. The Raging Battle

1. Homer, *The Iliad*, translated by Robert Fagles (New York: Penguin Books: 1990), Book 1, lines 193–198, pp. 82–83.

2. Ibid., Book 1, 241–242, 254.

3. Ibid., Book 1, 262–263.

4. Ibid., Book 16, lines 33–34, 40–47, p. 413.

5. Ibid., Book 18, lines 92–96 and 105–108, p. 470.

6. Ibid., Book 18, lines 140–150, p. 471.

7. Ibid., Book 18, lines 709–714.

8. Ibid., Book 19, lines 19–20.

9. Ibid., Book 19, lines 74–78.

10. Ibid., Book 19, lines 155–56, p. 495.

11. Ibid., Book 22, lines 407–418, p. 553.

12. Ibid., Book 24, lines 590–591, p. 605.

13. Christopher Marlowe, *The Tragical History of Dr. Faustus, 1604*; online at http://www.online-literature.com/marlowe/dr-faustus-1604/1/

Chapter 5. The End of Achilles

1. Homer, *The Odyssey,* translated by Robert Fitzgerald (New York: Farrar, Strauss and Giroux, 1988), Book 11, lines 578–582, p. 201.

For Young Adults

Fontes, Ron, and Justine. *The Trojan Horse: The Fall of Troy: A Greek Legend*. Minneapolis, Minnesota: Graphic Universe, 2006.

Hoena, B.A. *Odysseus*. Mankato, Minnesota: Capstone Press, 2006.

Horowitz, Anthony. *Myths and Legends*. Wilmington, Massachusetts: Kingfisher Books, 2003.

McCaughrean, Geraldine. *Greek Heroes*. New York: Oxford University Press, 2007.

Mabie, Hamilton Wright, editor. *Myths Every Child Should Know: A Selection of the Classic Myths of All Times for Young People*. Whitefish, Montana: Kessinger Publishing, 2003.

Verniero, Joan C, editor. *An Illustrated Treasury of Read-Aloud Myths and Legends: More than 40 of the World's Best-Loved Myths and Legends*. New York: Black Dog and Leventhal Publishers, 2004.

Works Consulted

Clarke, Lindsay. *The War at Troy*. New York: Thomas Dunne Books, 2004.

Cotterell, Arthur. *Classical Mythology*. New York: Lorenz Books, 2000.

Day, Malcolm. *100 Characters from Classical Mythology: Discover the Fascinating Stories of the Greek and Roman Deities*. New York: Barron's Educational Series, 2007.

Forty, Jo, editor. *Classic Mythology*. California: Thunder Bay Press, 1999.

Grant, Michael. *Who's Who in Classical Mythology*. London, England: Routledge, 2001.

Graves, Robert. *New Larousse Encyclopedia of Mythology*. London, England: Prometheus Press, 1968.

Hamilton, Edith. *Mythology: Timeless Tales of Gods and Heroes*. Boston: Back Bay Books, 1998.

Homer. *The Iliad*. Translated by Robert Fagles. New York: Penguin Books, 1990.

Homer. *The Odyssey*. Translated by Robert Fitzgerald. New York: Farrar, Strauss and Giroux, 1988.

Marlowe, Christopher. *The Tragical History of Dr. Faustus, 1604*; online at http://www.online-literature.com/marlowe/dr-faustus-1604/1/

Moncrieff, A.R. Hope. *Classic Myths and Legends*. London, England: Gresham Publishing Company, undated.

Statius. *Achilleid*. Translated by J. H. Mozley. Loeb Classical Library. Cambridge, Massachusetts: Harvard University Press; London: William Heinemann Ltd., 1928. Online at http://www.theoi.com/Text/StatiusAchilleid1A.html

Van Wees, Hans. *Greek Warfare: Myths and Realities*. London, England: Duckworth Publishers, 2004.

On the Internet

Ancient Greece: Art
www.ancient-greece.org/art.html

Ancient Greece—Art and Architecture, Sculpture, Pottery, and Greek Temples
www.ancientgreece.com/s/Art/

Encyclopedia of Greek Mythology: "Achilles"
http://www.mythweb.com/encyc/entries/achilles.html

Greek Mythology Link: Achilles
http://homepage.mac.com/cparada/GML/Achilles.html

Hunter, James. "Achilles." *Encyclopedia Mythica*.
http://www.pantheon.org/articles/a/achilles.html

Leadbetter, Ron. "Hephaestus." *Encyclopedia Mythica*.
http://www.pantheon.org/articles/h/hephaestus.html

Achilles and Ajax play checkers

ambrosia (am-BROH-zjuh)—Something delicious to taste or smell, often considered the food of the gods.

banished (BAA-nisht)—Sent away permanently.

centaurs (SEN-tars)—Mythical creatures that were half human (top) and half horse (bottom).

constellation (kon-stuh-LAY-shun)—A grouping of stars.

deity (DAY-ih-tee)—A god or goddess.

discord (DIS-kord)—Disagreement or dispute.

Hades (HAY-deez)—The Underworld, where souls of the dead live.

invulnerable (in-VOL-nuh-ruh-bul)—Incapable of being wounded or hurt.

mortal (MOR-tul)—Able to die.

myths (MITHS)—Stories or beliefs of a culture that help explain their world.

nymph (NIMF)—A beautiful maiden goddess that lives in the sea, woods, mountains, or other natural setting.

oracle (OR-uh-kul)—A person who speaks for a deity.

prophet (PRAH-fet)—A person who tells important information, often about the future.

pyre (PYR)—A pile or heap of wood for burning a dead body.

ransomed (RAN-sumd)—Asked for money in exchange for releasing a prisoner.

suitors (SOO-turs)—Traditionally, men who are interested in marrying a woman.

tendon (TEN-den)—A tough, fibrous tissue that connects a muscle to a bone.

trinket (TRING-ket)—A small ornament or piece of jewelry, usually of little value.